Your Marketing Plan awaits...

Available Now!

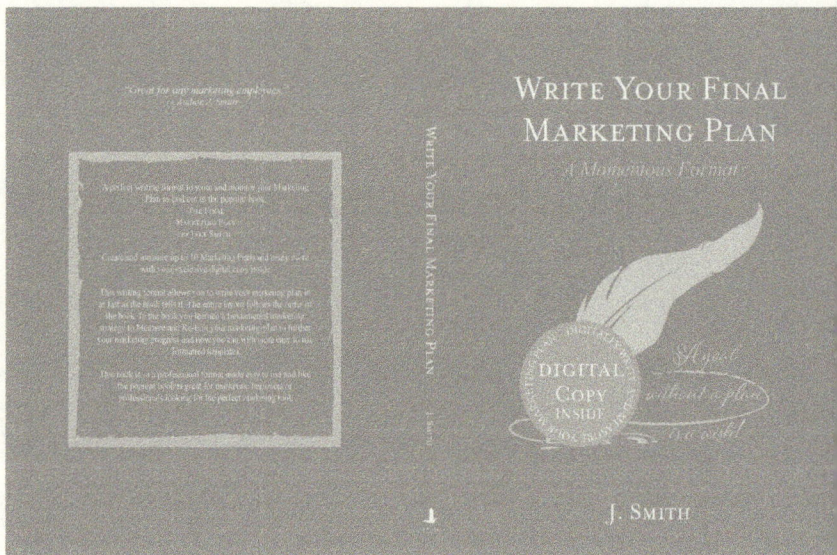

Get the matching writing template for the Final Marketing Plan you'll learn.

Preview on page 53

THE

A goal without a plan is a wish!

FINAL

MARKETING

PLAN

A Momentous Manual

J. SMITH

LAMP & SEA GROUP
2018

First Printing: 2018

ISBN 978-0692173237

Lamp & Sea Group
www.TheFinalMarketingPlan.com

For all who've inspired this work.

Always Remember

"There's little chances for success using people whom you *think* will buy your product versus <u>people whom you've discovered</u> will buy your product." (p. 4, Step 1.1)

Spread the word by sharing or tagging a book page.

share what you think is important

Contents

Preface

In order to accomplish creating the most precise and accurate description for all marketing strategies most privately published material that's associated with a strategy was not ignored.

The orchestration of this book allows you to complete an entire Marketing Plan using *all* the fundamental marketing strategies that are in existence. The book setup is convenient where you can easily pick-up where you left off at anytime, its all laid out with a series of chronological steps.

As intended this book also simultaneously doubles as a marketing manual for quickly looking up any marketing strategies outlined in the Contents page.

Introduction

This book was produced to showcase all the Fundamental Marketing Strategies which are as follows: Analyze the Population, Engage the Population, Analyze Consumer Buying Point, Pricing Strategy, Budgeting, and Evaluating/Re-writing the Marketing Plan.

All the Fundamental Marketing Strategies are included through a platform of 7 Steps, complete the first step to go on to the next and so forth. Step 7 is the last step and signifies the completion of *your entire Marketing Plan.*

By the end of this book you will have the knowledge to extrapolate an exact marketing strategy you ever known. For example, by the end of Step 4 you will become able to identify the marketing strategy that was used in a successful marketing campaign that took place in the United States known as: "Got Milk?."

You will find that this book doubles as a reference manual for marketing strategies and is useful for marketing beginners and experts alike. If you are very content with this book there is a leap of faith that you will help someone find their answers to marketing.

Step 1

Determine Your Target Customer

Unless your product (goods or services) fits under a very narrow niche you'll always have multiple different Target Customer profiles.

It's crucial to understand that people do not fit under one characteristic which is why broad and generic marketing generally don't convert well. A successful marketing always resonates with the Target Customer. So it's critical that you make your Target Customer as specific as possible so that you can craft the most personalized content.

Before being guided to obtain the interest of your Target Customer you'll need to create one. Use one Target Customer profile at a time when going through all steps.

Step 1.1

<u>Create Your Target Customer(s)</u>

Your Target Customer is a profile of the people whom you think or whom you've discovered will buy your product. There's little chances for success using people whom you *think* will buy your product versus <u>people whom you've *discovered*</u> will buy your product.

Create a Target Customer Profile then repeat the process to have a minimum of 2 or more different Target Customer Profiles—for one product. The last step, Step 7, will go over allocating funds after comparing a performance of a Target Customer Profile.

Keep in mind the more Target Customer Profiles you use the more Ad Space locations you will need.

Follow Rule # 1 below before answering the questions to create your Target Customer Profile.

Rule # 1:

Use only one Target Customer Profile at a time when following the rest of the Steps in this book.

Target Customer Profile

Age range?:

Sex?:

Geographic location(s) for work, home and pastime activities?:

Income?:

Marital Status?:

Occupation?:

Step 2

Determine When Customers Will Buy

Crucial to being successful in your marketing efforts is to identify your Customer's buying process. The more accurate you are with identifying their buying process the higher the chances you will have at being successful.

Use the following to identify your Target Customer's buying process then continue the steps to create Ad Texts.

Step 2.1

High-involvement Purchase Decision

Is when a purchase decision is considered a high "risk"

to your Target Customer because of one or any combined reasons as simply put by Silbiger (2012, p. 9):

"1. A high price

2. A need for the product's benefit to work (E.g., reliability—such as a pacemaker)

3. A need for the product's psychological reward to work (E.g., status, love)"

Solution To High-involvement Purchase

1. *A high price*

Design an Ad Text that describes a Money Back Guarantee. A Money Back Guarantee will take away the high price "risk" factor which is nothing more than a Target Customer not willing to pay what they consider a high amount if they are unsure of the product's effectiveness.

2. *A need for the product's benefit to work*

Design the Ad Text that describes why the product will work.

3. *A need for the product's psychological reward to work*

Design the Ad Text that describes an improved Social status, Mental status, or Bargain/Value.

Additional Solution For #s 1-2

Design an Ad Text for Branding/ Buyers Remorse to explain the value of your product. (p. 23, Step 4.6)

Step 2.2

Low-involvement Purchase Decision

Is a purchase decision that is considered a low "risk" to your Target Customer and they are more willing to buy your product because of one or all three reasons:

1. A low price

2. A lowered importance for the product's benefit to work

3. A lowered importance for the product's psychological reward benefit to work

Step 2.3

<u>Compulsive Buying</u>

The customer is more willing to buy because of one or all two reasons:

1. They view your advertisement in a time where the content is fully relatable to their current state.

2. Your product is readily accessible and available for purchase at a very convenient time for them.

Step 3

Determine How To Price Your Product

It's imperative to use your Target Customer Profile, created in Step 1, when analyzing the best pricing strategy to use. You will only use one pricing strategy at a time. The length of your pricing strategy will only be 1 to 2 months before measuring the pricing strategy effectiveness.

Step 3.1

<u>Perceived Value Pricing</u>

When you charge customers a price based on the value of the product. For example, eating popcorn at a movie theatre holds increased value over eating popcorn at home, therefore prices should be higher for popcorn to match the value of popcorn being eaten while watching a box office movie on a big screen.

Step 3.2

Perceived Quality Pricing

Perceived quality of products are always judged by its price, in which the higher the price the higher the perceived quality of the product. Notate customer's buying process before selecting any pricing strategy, especially for this one.

Step 3.3

Undercutting Competitor Pricing

Is to undercut the competitor's prices by offering same products of equal or better quality for a lower price.

Step 3.4

Inelastic Demand Pricing

This strategy is to continuously increase the price little by little because your customer's demand for your product is in such that they do not change their quantity purchases because of a price increase.

The opposite would be a customer who has an *elastic demand* for your product in such where continuous little by little price increases will effect if they continue buying your product or perhaps buying less quantities of your product. This usually is due to a customer's personal income, less desire for your product, or threshold for how much they are willing to spend for the type of product that your product is.

Step 3.5

Promotions and Rewards

Use your Target Customer to select the best promotion and reward offerings to be used in conjunction with a pricing strategy.

Coupon Promotions

To incentivize a Target Customer you can create coupon or sample offers. The more *significant* of a discount or perhaps a free product that you're able to offer then the greater the incentive you'll create.

Example:

A hardware store chain currently gains significant success by always offering coupons in their monthly mail advertisements for one free item *without* purchase.

The free item is always a universally recognizable brand name and is a product such as a measuring tape, flashlight, hammer, etc. The free item value always equals to a $8-$14 value. Importantly they are always able to supply everyone having a coupon with the free item throughout the coupon activation period (usually a 3-4 weeks span).

If you are unable to supply everyone with a coupon it will cause your future coupons to loose incentive as more and more people become aware that your coupon carries odds on successfully working.

Loyalty Rewards and Membership Programs

In general, you do not want to have a <u>loyalty reward</u> and a <u>membership program</u> *running* at the same time, because one of the two offerings is going to be *the* better value or both offerings will equal the same value and a customer will question your entire business integrity for having a lesser offering value or two offerings that equals the same value. This will cause you to loose customers trust.

Loyalty Rewards

Incentivizing current customers to keep using your products can be done by offering discounts or free products when your customer has made a certain number of purchases. The higher the discount, the higher the *significance* or value of the discount or free product thus the greater the incentive to keep buying your product.

Membership Programs

You will always have greater membership sign-ups if the new consumers first use your product before offering them a valuable membership program. Never offer customers to use your product for free, at minimum always offer at least the expense it costs you to produce the product. Otherwise you will create a <u>lowered perceived </u>value of your product and an accumulation of debt. The higher the value/ *significance* of a membership price the greater the incentive you give customers.

Referral Rewards

For some businesses the vast majority of their successes

has been by word of mouth. If you decide to incentivize a customer to talk about your product with whom people they know then the most effective method is to offer a referral reward. This means to offer something free that is a part of your product.

Incentivizing the potential customer who is being referred, by offering them the same reward with equal or greater value, is a great way to persuade them to use your product for the first time.

Step 3.6

A/B Split Test For Pricing Strategy

Allow 1 to 2 months to go by before creating a second version for your pricing strategy. Use one strategy at a time. After allowing 2 to 4 months for two pricing strategies keep re-use the strategy that produced the most profit (Profit = Revenue minus Expense). Repeat this process again to continue having the best pricing strategy for your product.

Step 4

Create Advertising Text

It's critical for your Advertising Text to cater individually to your Target Customer. Follow Rules # 1-5 when answering the following questions to create specific Advertising Texts (Ad Texts).

Rule # 1:

Use Layman's Terms: A style of communication that uses easy to understand plain language with an emphasis on clarity and the avoidance of overly complex vocabulary. Keep in mind that less is more in order to obtain a Target Customer's attention.

Rule # 2:

Write out your Advertising Text the instant you think of it, after you read each question and do not worry if it's a long answer because you can always go back to the Ad Text later. However nothing could be revisited if nothing is written. Writer's block usually occurs if you attempt to make you first answer perfect.

Rule # 3:

Revise your Ad Text 2 to 3 times to: sound better, be shortened, and/or if necessary be split up into two or more separated Ad Texts.

Rule # 4:

Use only one Target Customer Profile at a time to create your Ad Text from the given questions.

Rule # 5:

Afterward, review your finished Ad Texts to decide which one/s you will create a design/content for and use. Start out by choosing the most relatable Ad Text to all or majority of your Target Customers.

Step 4.1

Social Acceptance Advertising Text

Create Advertising Texts that targets your customer's emotions on being socially accepted by members and/or groups of their peers.

Peers can be co-workers, friends, or anyone else they interact with. Peers will also be the population that your Target Customer wants to be associated with or a person they desire to have a romantic relationship with.

What makes your product cause your Target Customer's peers to look up to

them? Ad Text:

What makes your product fix or keep your Target Customer's relationship/s? (Include the relationship.) Ad Text:

What makes your product cause your Target Customer's peers to be more attracted to them? (E.g., girlfriend, etc.) Ad Text:

Step 4.2

Health/Well Being Advertising Text

Create Advertising Texts that targets your customer's emotions about their specific health/well being.

What *physical* health issue does all or majority of your Target Customer base have and what makes your product improve it? Ad Text:

What *mental* health issue does all or majority of your Target Customer base have and what makes your product improve it? Ad Text:

Step 4.3

<u>Competitor Advertising Text</u>

Create Advertising Texts that targets your customer's skepticism of using your product versus a more established company.

What makes your product's physical appearance better than your competitors? Ad Text:

What makes your product have better quality than your competitors? Ad Text:

What makes your product have better effectiveness than your competitors? Ad Text:

What makes using your product versus your competitors a consumers advantage (a better value)? Ad Text:

Step 4.4

Niche Expert Advertising Text

Create Advertising Texts that targets your customer's desire for a *'guaranteed-to-work'* solution to their problem.

What existing problem does all or majority of your Target Customer base have and what makes your product guarantee to solve it? Ad Text:

Step 4.5

Lifestyle Advertising Text

Create Advertising Texts that targets your customer's desire to have a specific experience.

What type of experience does all or majority of your Target Customer base want to have and what makes your product provide it? Ad Text:

Step 4.6

<u>Branding/Buyers Remorse Advertising Text</u>

Create Advertising Texts that targets your customer's thought process on how they feel after paying for your product. Give answers to any of their second guessing thoughts. The purpose is to make them want to return versus going elsewhere.

What is one expectation that all or majority of your Target Customer base have for your product and what makes your product guarantee to delivery that expectation? (Include the expectation.) Ad Text:

What is one detailed feeling your previous customers all have after using your product? Ad Text:

What makes your product hard to be complained about after your customers use it? Ad Text:

Step 4.7

A/B Split Test Strategy For Ad Text

Create two versions for an Ad Text. Use both Ad Text versions either at the same time or at different times. Keep the Ad Text version that produced the most profit then create/use a new Ad Text content version to repeat the performance comparison process over again.

Step 4.8

Reverse Psychology Version For Ad Text

Create another version of an already fully revised Ad Text that will tell your Target Customer they do not need to use your product for the reason given in the Ad Text.

Include the original Ad Text when creating the Reverse Psychology version, a perfect example is to add the phrase "DO NOT HAVE" to your Ad Text:

Sample

Original Ad Text

Have a good time tonight by drinking our hydrating drink.

Reverse Psychology Ad Text

You DO NOT HAVE to have a good time tonight by drinking our hydrating drink.

Step 5

Create Ad Design For Advertising Text

In order to acquire favorable marketing results you will need to replace your Ad Texts with an image or video content. Creating the right content to clearly define an Ad Text is crucial to your marketing efforts and is the only way to get optimal results.

Use the following to create a content and a design layout for all Ad Text(s).

Step 5.1

Photographs versus Art Illustrations

People will always be able to better picture themselves in the context of a photograph versus any art illustration. Thus in comparison creating a photograph to clearly define an Ad Text will always be more appealing.

Step 5.2

Video versus Photograph

A video that clearly defines an Ad Text is significantly more effective than any photograph. Video clips combine visual and audio as well as a special ability to host several different Ad Texts in a single video clip. Note: Mobile video traffic is to grow 55% each year until 2020.

Step 5.3

Creating Video Clips

Resource To Edit Videos

Adobe Premier or Mobile Apps

Video content must clearly define your chosen Ad Text in as minimal time as possible: 8-15 seconds—includes the runtime for the logo and product or contact information. This is due to the shorten attention span of people who are already over saturated with other media online (and offline).

If you chosen to try hosting several different Ad Texts in a single video clip you must allow additional 8-15 seconds for each Ad Text.

Keep in mind it's best to create video content for one Ad Text at a time making tan entire video clip only 8-15 seconds long because of the shorten attention span of people who are experiencing high volumes of content.

Step 5.4

<u>Creating Photographs</u>

Resource To Edit Photographs

Adobe Illustrator or Mobile Apps

In order to clearly define your Ad Text the photograph must be created from scratch otherwise it will be too boring and ineffective if using just an internet stock image. The creation of a new photograph is also required in order to clearly define your custom tailored Ad Text.

Critical to making your photographs more appealing is using the right grid theories (may also be used with video and art illustrations). The following are two grid theories showcased with demonstrated samples.

Follow two rules when using a grid theory to create a photograph.

Rule # 1:

The way a grid theory works is by laying

all the objects, focal points, logos and contact information along the lines of a grid. This in turn will make the items more appealing and get people to look the photograph.

There is one exception: placing objects inside any one of the smallest boxes for The Phi Grid theory is necessary in order to make the areas that are in the box more appealing as you will see in a sample photograph on the next page.

Do not place your Logo in the small boxes as it will be too small in comparison to the size of the overall photograph.

Rule # 2:

Always DELETE the GRID/GRID LINES before using the finalized content.

The Phi Grid

This is used for more subtle presentations of objects versus the following Rule Of Thirds Grid. This Phi Grid is great for landscape photography as it makes objects look more natural and/or more subtle than dramatic.

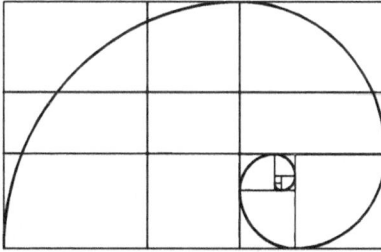

Samples:

The Rule Of Thirds Grid

This is used for more dramatic presentations of objects versus the previous Phi Grid. This Rule Of Thirds Grid is great for object photography as it makes objects look more dramatic and/or more obvious.

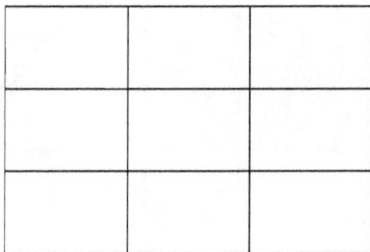

Samples:

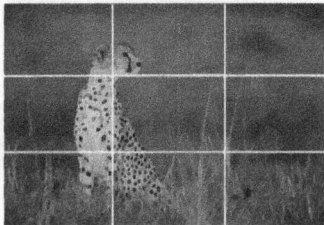

Step 5.5

Choose Colors For Photos/Videos & Illustrations

It's crucial to choose the right colors for your content based on the meaning of what each color represents. Use only the colors that help define your chosen Ad Text. Select from the following list of colors and their meanings.

Grey:

> Conveys neutrality and thus often found in backgrounds; has no significant depth to make a difference alone.

Black:

> Suggests authority, strength, elegance, power, and prestige.

White:

> Stands for purity, goodness, cleanliness, precision, and perfection.

Purple:

Represents wealth, power, comfort, extravagance, magic, mystery, and spirituality.

Blue:

Indicates integrity, trust, importance, confidence, and stability.

Green:

Symbolizes growth, healthiness, harmony, blooming, and healing, and often is associated with safety or money.

Yellow:

Suggests sunshine, happiness, hope, liveliness, and intelligence.

Orange:

Denotes success, victory, creativity, and enthusiasm.

Brown:

> Represents simplicity, honesty, and
> dependability.

Red:

> Expresses danger, power, or energy, and often
> is associated with sports or physical exertion.

Step 5.6

Memorable Design Layouts For Advertising Text

A memorable design layout yields the greatest amount of marketing results. Your content must have the upmost _simplicity_ and _strength_ (very clear definition of the Ad Text). Follow two rules when designing a _memorable design layout:_

Rule # 1:

> Include your Logo and/or brief contact

information. If your ad becomes memorable but your brand or product cannot be remembered with it then your ad was not effective and better off not existing.

Rule # 2:

If it proves to be impossible to *clearly define* your chosen Ad Text with only imagery content then you may include as few words as possible into the content. Remember to place words along a grid theory line to make it more appealing. Note: The more words used the less effectiveness the ad will have.

Step 5.7

<u>Elegant Design Layouts For Advertising Text</u>

An elegant design layout produces less results than the *memorable design layout*. To create this layout start by using 2 or 3 Ad Text photographs to define one Ad Text and lay them out in a comic-strip like fashion. Use no words to connect the photographs; unless absolutely vital in order to help clearly define the Ad Text.

Step 5.8

<u>Product and Price Display Design Layout</u>

A product and price display design layout produces the least amount of favorable results—if any. This design layout is created by displaying an array of products with their respective prices.

This layout is not appealing to the eye hence does not capture the attention span of people nor does it target an emotion or feeling they can associate with.

Campaigning Your Ad Design Layouts

You must use a campaign in order to increase favorable results. To create a campaign simple start by using 2 or more Ad Text photographs and/or video clips that are linked to each other by a single concept (e.g., love, friendship, career, pets, love for wine, etc.). The Ads must run simultaneously on different Ad delivery locations/Ad Spaces—covered in the next step. First follow two rules when creating your campaign concept.

Rule # 1:

> The concept you will link between different Ads *must be easily recognizable* to your Target Customer.

Rule # 2:

> Always include your Logo and/or brief contact information for every Ad you create, like the campaign concept your Logos *must be easily recognizable* to your Target Customer.

Step 5.10

A/B Split Test Strategy For Ad Design Layouts

Create two Ad Design Layout versions for one Ad Text. Use both Ad Design versions either at the same time or at different times. Keep the Ad Design version that produced the most profit then create new Ad Design to repeat the process over again.

Use this same A/B Split Test Strategy for your Campaign Concept.

Step 6

Where To Deliver Ad Designs

It's vital to keep in mind that you do not want to be too frequent with your ads because of the risk of turning your audiences off, thus using 1 to 2 Ads per Ad Space/ad location should be your limit. You also do not want to be no more frequent than one week when changing ads for an ad location, as you will learn in Step 7 under *Ad Runtimes*.

Step 6.1

<u>Free Ad Space</u>

Your Business Location

Places in or around your business property that can be visible to foot and/or vehicle traffic. *Ad Space:*

Social Media

Create the same social media account that all or majority of your Target Customer base use. Individually send them requests to follow you so they can view your Ad posts and/or use #Hashtags in your posts to bring more exposure to them.

Step 7 will further explain that one week is the minimum Ad Space run time before posting another Ad Design on your social media account. Additionally, 1 Ad Design post at a time per social media account should be your limitation. *Ad Space:*

Hashtags On Social Media and Blogs

#Hashtags connect your social media or blog posts to other posts that people upload whom attached the same #Hashtags to their posts as you. You'll want to make sure you select the most popular #Hashtags and not your own (E.g., company name, etc.).

Instagram for example when you begin to type the # symbol it automatically starts showing you suggested #Hashtags listed with their popularity.

#Hashtags allow you to designate posts as being part of a particular conversation that all or majority of your Target Customers are involved in.

When creating a #Hashtag for a social media or blog account make sure that your hashtags are one word, even if it's a two- or three- word idea hence if you create a #Hashtag using #my hashtag, the word "my" is the only word that will actually be tagged/attached to the post.

It's critical not to start a hashtag for your own company or product because of how extremely and noticeably desperate the act will look like to your followers.

You're generally allowed to use multiple different #Hashtags in one post. Keep in mind your #Hashtags are visible to all viewers of your post.

Step 6.2

Paid Ad Space

Travel Route Ads

What specific transportation route does all or majority of your Target Customer base use. List any street or highway names and check for available Ad Spaces along that path (E.g., large billboards, etc.). *Ad Space:*

Media Ads

What specific media such as Newspapers, Magazines or online sites does all or majority of your Target Customers base use? *Ad Space:*

Establishments

What establishment does all or majority of your Target Customer base frequent? (E.g., family restaurant, spas, movie theaters, retail stores, etc.) If the establishment does not have available advertisement spaces you can opt to search for ad spaces nearby the establishment. *Ad Space:*

Social Media and Apps

What Social Media or Apps do all or majority of your Target Customer base use? This could be YouTube, Instagram, etc. The respective chosen sites will have information for posting paid ads on their platform. *Ad Space:*

T.V. Cable

What T.V. cable programs do all or majority of your Target Customer base watch? This is for a high costing commercial air time that is only worth it if you have the correct Target Customer base and correct T.V. program they are into. *Ad Space:*

Events

What events does all or majority of your Target Customer base frequent? This could be charity walks, concerts, tech conventions, business conventions, community farmer's markets, etc. Well organized events will usually charge a fee to set-up a booth. *Ad Space:*

In-Person

What location does all or majority of your Target Customer base frequent? This is so that you can meet them in person with your products in hand to give a short demonstration about your product. This is what gives smaller businesses a competitive edge over bigger and more established companies whom do not have the resources to personally meet their Target Customers wherever their products are sold. *Ad Space:*

Step 7

Measuring/Re-Editing Marketing Plan

It's crucial to measure the Revenue and Expense of an Ad to allow a chance to allocate more marketing funds into the Ad that is performing the highest. Respectively you can reduce marketing costs by eliminating low or non-performing ads.

By measuring each Ads performance periodically before the Ads runtime you chosen has ended you can be able to eliminate an Ad early before it could acquire any more expense than revenue.

Step 7.1

Set Ad Runtimes

Every Ad you use should have a length of how long you it will run. The Ad and Ad Space must be seen as a whole. Runtime lengths must be any of the following: one Week, one Month, one Quarter (3 Months), or one Year.

Step 7.2

Measuring the Ad Revenue

The company's revenue during an ad's runtime becomes the Ad Revenue for the ad. If there are multiple ads for the same ad runtime then the company's revenue results should be evenly disbursed to list each Ad Revenue. The only time you will not evenly disburse revenue results is for very rare occasions that you are able to determine the ad that generated each sale.

Step 7.3

Profitable Ad

Occurs when the total revenue gained from the Ad (and its Ad Space) is *greater* than the overall cost for the Ad (and its Ad Space). If you use the A/B split test strategy and run two different versions of the same ad you will then eliminate the lower profit producing ad to make room for another variation of the same ad.

Step 7.4

Unprofitable Ad

Occurs when the total revenue gained from the Ad /Ad Space is *lesser* than the overall cost for the Ad (and its Ad Space). You can use the A/B split test strategy to reuse an ad with at least one aspect or step process about it being different.

Keep in mind that even economical spending on low costing Ads will be wasted if it's not the proper delivery location that reaches enough of your Target Customer to make profit over the cost of the ad delivery location.

Step 7.5

<u>Determine Where To Spread Costs</u>

Create a list with the total revenue and expenses   for each Ad during its runtime then calculate the profit acquired from having the Ad (Profit = Revenue minus Expense).

Simply use your current Marketing Budget to increase spending on your higher profitable Ads and decrease or eliminate spending on your least profitable or completely unprofitable ads. Critical to your marketing is continuously adjusting your budget for each Ad.

How Much To Spend On Marketing

On average companies will spend **13 percent** of their annual revenue on overall marketing activities.

Additionally, its better to view your marketing costs as an investment versus expense to show that you are seeking a return on an investment rather than just accruing costs for no reason.

Step 7.6

<u>Measuring Pricing Strategy</u>

Measuring *Total Ad Profits* for the duration of your pricing strategy is used to measure the results of the pricing strategy—as such *Ad Profits* already includes your sales/ revenue.

KINDLY SHARE YOUR
THOUGHTS

REVIEW WITH ANY ONLINE BOOK
RETAILERS OR COMMUNITY SITES

Preview on NEXT PAGE From

Write Your Final Marketing Plan

By J. Smith

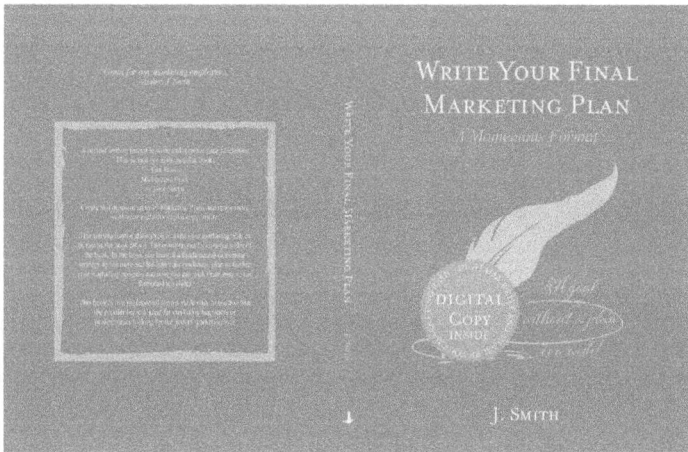

Write and measure up to 10 printed marketing plans and receive the Digital Copy *downloads: PDF and/or Excel.*

Book Preview—**Guide For Using Format**

For Pricing Strategy

<u>Create more item boxes</u>

Double item boxes by using a straight object (E.g., ruler) to draw a line horizontally across so that one item box turns into two item boxes, this method allows up to 26 total item boxes.

For Complete Ads

<u>Use 1 Target Customer per Campaign Concept</u>

Have more than one Ad visible from the same campaign

concept per Target Customer.

__Select 1 Target Customer that best represents each Ad out of the Target Customers you create__

Personalized content is crucial to acquire any success otherwise the ad was better off never existing. For each Marketing Plan template you are given the option to create 6 Target Customers but can only use one that best represents a Target Ad.

Solution to use more than one Target Customer for one Ad

To use more than one Target Customer to represent the same **Complete Ad** you can fill out additional marketing plans. A second option would be to use the Digital Copy of the Marketing Plan template to create more of the same Ads for different Target Customers.

Marketing Plan

1

Target Customer Profile

⌐ ¦ Complete Repeat from Marketing Plan #_____

Target Customer # 1	Age Range	Sex	Income
Marital Status	Occupation	Geographic location(s) for work	
Geographic location(s) for home		Geographic location(s) for pastime activities	

Target Customer # 2	Age Range	Sex	Income
Marital Status	Occupation	Geographic location(s) for work	
Geographic location(s) for home		Geographic location(s) for pastime activities	

Target Customer # 3	Age Range	Sex	Income
Marital Status	Occupation	Geographic location(s) for work	
Geographic location(s) for home		Geographic location(s) for pastime activities	

Target Customer # 4	Age Range	Sex	Income
Marital Status	Occupation	Geographic location(s) for work	
Geographic location(s) for home		Geographic location(s) for pastime activities	

Target Customer # 5	Age Range	Sex	Income
Marital Status	Occupation	Geographic location(s) for work	
Geographic location(s) for home		Geographic location(s) for pastime activities	

Target Customer # 6	Age Range	Sex	Income
Marital Status	Occupation	Geographic location(s) for work	
Geographic location(s) for home		Geographic location(s) for pastime activities	

Pricing Strategy

	Perceived Value	Price	Start Date	End Date	Total Ad Revenue	Total Ad Cost	Total Ad Profit
	All items (option)						
item							
item							
item							
item							
item							
item							

item						
item						
item						
item						
item						
item						
item						

⟨⟩	Perceived Quality	Price	Start Date	End Date	Total Ad Revenue	Total Ad Cost	Total Ad Profit
All items (option)							
i t e m							
i t e m							
i t e m							
i t e m							
i t e m							
i t e m							
i t e m							

item						
item						
item						
item						
item						
item						

☐	Undercutting Competitor	Price	Start Date	End Date	Total Ad Revenue	Total Ad Cost	Total Ad Profit
	All items (option)						
i t e m							
i t e m							
i t e m							
i t e m							
i t e m							
i t e m							
i t e m							

item					
item					
item					
item					
item					
item					

ॱ॑	Inelastic Demand	Price	Start Date	End Date	Total Ad Revenue	Total Ad Cost	Total Ad Profit
All items (option)							
i t e m							
i t e m							
i t e m							
i t e m							
i t e m							
i t e m							
i t e m							

item						
item						
item						
item						
item						
item						

⟲	Coupon Promotions	Price	Start Date	End Date	Total Ad Revenue	Total Ad Cost	Total Ad Profit
All items (option)							
i t e m							
i t e m							
i t e m							
i t e m							
i t e m							
i t e m							
i t e m							

item						
item						
item						
item						
item						
item						

☼	Loyalty Rewards	Price	Start Date	End Date	Total Ad Revenue	Total Ad Cost	Total Ad Profit
All items (option)							
i t e m							
i t e m							
i t e m							
i t e m							
i t e m							
i t e m							
i t e m							

item						
item						
item						
item						
item						
item						

⚙	Membership Programs	Price	Start Date	End Date	Total Ad Revenue	Total Ad Cost	Total Ad Profit
	All items (option)						
i t e m							
i t e m							
i t e m							
i t e m							
i t e m							
i t e m							
i t e m							

item					
item					
item					
item					
item					
item					

⸭	Referral Rewards	Price	Start Date	End Date	Total Ad Revenue	Total Ad Cost	Total Ad Profit
All items (option)							
i t e m							
i t e m							
i t e m							
i t e m							
i t e m							
i t e m							
i t e m							

item						
item						
item						
item						
item						
item						

Complete Ads

Social Acceptance	Photograph or Video:	Phi Grid or Rule Of Thirds:	Colors:	Memorable or Elegant Layout:
What makes your product cause your Target Customer's peers to look up to them?	Target Customer #	Ad Space Location		
		Total Revenue: Total Expense: Total Profit:		
Answer		Ad Space Location		
		Total Revenue: Total Expense: Total Profit:		
Revision		Ad Space Location		
		Total Revenue: Total Expense: Total Profit:		
Revision		Ad Space Location		
		Total Revenue: Total Expense: Total Profit:		

Revision	Ad Space Location
	Total Revenue: Total Expense: Total Profit:
Final Ad Text	Ad Space Location
	Total Revenue: Total Expense: Total Profit:
Reverse Psychology Version Instead	Computer: Ad Design File Name
Campaign Concept	Ad Runtime: Dates
#Hashtags	Ad Space For Used #Hashtags

Social Acceptance	Photograph or Video:	Phi Grid or Rule Of Thirds:	Colors:	Memorable or Elegant Layout:
What makes your product fix or keep your Target Customer's relationship/s? (Include the relationship.)	Target Customer #	Ad Space Location Total Revenue: Total Expense: Total Profit:		

Answer	Ad Space Location
	Total Revenue: Total Expense: Total Profit:

Revision	Ad Space Location
	Total Revenue: Total Expense: Total Profit:

Revision	Ad Space Location
	Total Revenue: Total Expense: Total Profit:

Revision	Ad Space Location
	Total Revenue: Total Expense: Total Profit:
Final Ad Text	Ad Space Location
	Total Revenue: Total Expense: Total Profit:
Reverse Psychology Version Instead	Computer: Ad Design File Name
Campaign Concept	Ad Runtime: Dates
#Hashtags	Ad Space For Used #Hashtags

Social Acceptance	Photograph or Video:	Phi Grid or Rule Of Thirds:	Colors:	Memorabl e or Elegant Layout:
What makes your product cause your Target Customer's peers to be more attracted to them? (E.g. girlfriend, etc.)	Target Customer #	Ad Space Location Total Revenue: Total Expense: Total Profit:		
Answer		Ad Space Location Total Revenue: Total Expense: Total Profit:		
Revision		Ad Space Location Total Revenue: Total Expense: Total Profit:		
Revision		Ad Space Location Total Revenue: Total Expense: Total Profit:		

Revision	Ad Space Location
	Total Revenue: Total Expense: Total Profit:
Final Ad Text	Ad Space Location
	Total Revenue: Total Expense: Total Profit:
Reverse Psychology Version Instead	Computer: Ad Design File Name
Campaign Concept	Ad Runtime: Dates
#Hashtags	Ad Space For Used #Hashtags

⌂ **Health/Well Being**	Photograph or Video:	Phi Grid or Rule Of Thirds:	Colors:	Memorable or Elegant Layout:
What *physical* health issue does all or majority of your Target Customer base have and what makes your product improve it?	Target Customer #	Ad Space Location		
		Total Revenue: Total Expense: Total Profit:		
Answer		Ad Space Location		
		Total Revenue: Total Expense: Total Profit:		
Revision		Ad Space Location		
		Total Revenue: Total Expense: Total Profit:		
Revision		Ad Space Location		
		Total Revenue: Total Expense: Total Profit:		

Revision	Ad Space Location
	Total Revenue: Total Expense: Total Profit:
Final Ad Text	Ad Space Location
	Total Revenue: Total Expense: Total Profit:
Reverse Psychology Version Instead	Computer: Ad Design File Name
Campaign Concept	Ad Runtime: Dates
#Hashtags	Ad Space For Used #Hashtags

Health/Well Being	Photograph or Video:	Phi Grid or Rule Of Thirds:	Colors:	Memorable or Elegant Layout:
What *mental* health issue does all or majority of your Target Customer base have and what makes your product improve it?	Target Customer #	Ad Space Location Total Revenue: Total Expense: Total Profit:		

Answer	Ad Space Location
	Total Revenue: Total Expense: Total Profit:

Revision	Ad Space Location
	Total Revenue: Total Expense: Total Profit:

Revision	Ad Space Location
	Total Revenue: Total Expense: Total Profit:

Revision	Ad Space Location
	Total Revenue: Total Expense: Total Profit:
Final Ad Text	Ad Space Location
	Total Revenue: Total Expense: Total Profit:
Reverse Psychology Version Instead	Computer: Ad Design File Name
Campaign Concept	Ad Runtime: Dates
#Hashtags	Ad Space For Used #Hashtags

Competitor Advertising	Photograph or Video:	Phi Grid or Rule Of Thirds:	Colors:	Memorable or Elegant Layout:
What makes your product's physical appearance better than your competitors?	Target Customer #	Ad Space Location		
		Total Revenue: Total Expense: Total Profit:		

Answer   Ad Space Location

Total Revenue:
Total Expense:
Total Profit:

Revision   Ad Space Location

Total Revenue:
Total Expense:
Total Profit:

Revision   Ad Space Location

Total Revenue:
Total Expense:
Total Profit:

Revision	Ad Space Location
	Total Revenue: Total Expense: Total Profit:
Final Ad Text	Ad Space Location
	Total Revenue: Total Expense: Total Profit:
Reverse Psychology Version Instead	Computer: Ad Design File Name
Campaign Concept	Ad Runtime: Dates
#Hashtags	Ad Space For Used #Hashtags

Competitor Advertising	Photograph or Video:	Phi Grid or Rule Of Thirds:	Colors:	Memorable or Elegant Layout:
What makes your product have better quality than your competitors?	Target Customer #	Ad Space Location		
		Total Revenue: Total Expense: Total Profit:		

Answer	Ad Space Location
	Total Revenue: Total Expense: Total Profit:

Revision	Ad Space Location
	Total Revenue: Total Expense: Total Profit:

Revision	Ad Space Location
	Total Revenue: Total Expense: Total Profit:

Revision	Ad Space Location
	Total Revenue: Total Expense: Total Profit:
Final Ad Text	Ad Space Location
	Total Revenue: Total Expense: Total Profit:
Reverse Psychology Version Instead	Computer: Ad Design File Name
Campaign Concept	Ad Runtime: Dates
#Hashtags	Ad Space For Used #Hashtags

Competitor Advertising	Photograph or Video:	Phi Grid or Rule Of Thirds:	Colors:	Memorabl e or Elegant Layout:
What makes your product have better effectiveness than your competitors?	Target Customer #	Ad Space Location		
		Total Revenue: Total Expense: Total Profit:		

Answer	Ad Space Location
	Total Revenue: Total Expense: Total Profit:

Revision	Ad Space Location
	Total Revenue: Total Expense: Total Profit:

Revision	Ad Space Location
	Total Revenue: Total Expense: Total Profit:

Revision	Ad Space Location
	Total Revenue: Total Expense: Total Profit:
Final Ad Text	Ad Space Location
	Total Revenue: Total Expense: Total Profit:
Reverse Psychology Version Instead	Computer: Ad Design File Name
Campaign Concept	Ad Runtime: Dates
#Hashtags	Ad Space For Used #Hashtags

	Competitor Advertising	Photograph or Video:	Phi Grid or Rule Of Thirds:	Colors:	Memorabl e or Elegant Layout:
What makes using your product versus your competitors a consumers advantage (a better value)?		Target Customer #	Ad Space Location		
			Total Revenue: Total Expense: Total Profit:		

Answer	Ad Space Location
	Total Revenue: Total Expense: Total Profit:

Revision	Ad Space Location
	Total Revenue: Total Expense: Total Profit:

Revision	Ad Space Location
	Total Revenue: Total Expense: Total Profit:

Revision	Ad Space Location
	Total Revenue: Total Expense: Total Profit:
Final Ad Text	Ad Space Location
	Total Revenue: Total Expense: Total Profit:
Reverse Psychology Version Instead	Computer: Ad Design File Name
Campaign Concept	Ad Runtime: Dates
#Hashtags	Ad Space For Used #Hashtags

Niche Expert	Photograph or Video:	Phi Grid or Rule Of Thirds:	Colors:	Memorable or Elegant Layout:
What existing problem does all or majority of your Target Customer base have and what makes your product guarantee to solve it?	Target Customer #	Ad Space Location Total Revenue: Total Expense: Total Profit:		
Answer		Ad Space Location Total Revenue: Total Expense: Total Profit:		
Revision		Ad Space Location Total Revenue: Total Expense: Total Profit:		
Revision		Ad Space Location Total Revenue: Total Expense: Total Profit:		

Revision	Ad Space Location
	Total Revenue: Total Expense: Total Profit:
Final Ad Text	Ad Space Location
	Total Revenue: Total Expense: Total Profit:
Reverse Psychology Version Instead	Computer: Ad Design File Name
Campaign Concept	Ad Runtime: Dates
#Hashtags	Ad Space For Used #Hashtags

Lifestyle Advertising	Photograph or Video:	Phi Grid or Rule Of Thirds:	Colors:	Memorable or Elegant Layout:
What type of experience does all or majority of your Target Customer base want to have and what makes your product provide it?	Target Customer #	Ad Space Location Total Revenue: Total Expense: Total Profit:		
Answer		Ad Space Location Total Revenue: Total Expense: Total Profit:		
Revision		Ad Space Location Total Revenue: Total Expense: Total Profit:		
Revision		Ad Space Location Total Revenue: Total Expense: Total Profit:		

Revision	Ad Space Location
	Total Revenue: Total Expense: Total Profit:
Final Ad Text	Ad Space Location
	Total Revenue: Total Expense: Total Profit:
Reverse Psychology Version Instead	Computer: Ad Design File Name
Campaign Concept	Ad Runtime: Dates
#Hashtags	Ad Space For Used #Hashtags

Branding/Buyers Remorse	Photograph or Video:	Phi Grid or Rule Of Thirds:	Colors:	Memorable or Elegant Layout:
What is one expectation that all or majority of your Target Customer base have for your product and what makes your product guarantee to delivery that expectation? (Include the expectation.)	Target Customer #	Ad Space Location Total Revenue: Total Expense: Total Profit:		
Answer		Ad Space Location Total Revenue: Total Expense: Total Profit:		
Revision		Ad Space Location Total Revenue: Total Expense: Total Profit:		
Revision		Ad Space Location Total Revenue: Total Expense: Total Profit:		

Revision	Ad Space Location
	Total Revenue: Total Expense: Total Profit:
Final Ad Text	Ad Space Location
	Total Revenue: Total Expense: Total Profit:
Reverse Psychology Version Instead	Computer: Ad Design File Name
Campaign Concept	Ad Runtime: Dates
#Hashtags	Ad Space For Used #Hashtags

Branding/Buyers Remorse	Photograph or Video:	Phi Grid or Rule Of Thirds:	Colors:	Memorable or Elegant Layout:
What is one detailed feeling your previous customers all have after using your product?	Target Customer #	Ad Space Location		
		Total Revenue: Total Expense: Total Profit:		
Answer		Ad Space Location		
		Total Revenue: Total Expense: Total Profit:		
Revision		Ad Space Location		
		Total Revenue: Total Expense: Total Profit:		
Revision		Ad Space Location		
		Total Revenue: Total Expense: Total Profit:		

Revision	Ad Space Location
	Total Revenue: Total Expense: Total Profit:
Final Ad Text	Ad Space Location
	Total Revenue: Total Expense: Total Profit:
Reverse Psychology Version Instead	Computer: Ad Design File Name
Campaign Concept	Ad Runtime: Dates
#Hashtags	Ad Space For Used #Hashtags

⌐⌐ **Branding/Buyers Remorse**	Photograph or Video:	Phi Grid or Rule Of Thirds:	Colors:	Memorab le or Elegant Layout:
What makes your product hard to be complained about after your customers use it?	Target Customer #	Ad Space Location Total Revenue: Total Expense: Total Profit:		
Answer		Ad Space Location Total Revenue: Total Expense: Total Profit:		
Revision		Ad Space Location Total Revenue: Total Expense: Total Profit:		
Revision		Ad Space Location Total Revenue: Total Expense: Total Profit:		

Revision	Ad Space Location
	Total Revenue: Total Expense: Total Profit:
Final Ad Text	Ad Space Location
	Total Revenue: Total Expense: Total Profit:
Reverse Psychology Version Instead	Computer: Ad Design File Name
Campaign Concept	Ad Runtime: Dates
#Hashtags	Ad Space For Used #Hashtags

End of Preview

Reference

Silbiger, S. (2012). *The Ten-Day MBA*. New York, NY: HarperCollins.